Up the Garden Path

Are you a
Bee?

KINGFISHER
Kingfisher Publications Plc
New Penderel House
283-288 High Holborn
London WC1V 7HZ

First published by Kingfisher Publications Plc 2001

1 3 5 7 9 10 8 6 4 2

production code

A CIP catalogue record for this book is available from
the British Library.

ISBN 0 7534 0539 3

Editors: Katie Puckett, Carron Brown
Series Designers: Jane Tassie, Jane Buckley

Printed in Singapore

Up the Garden Path

Are you a Bee?

Judy Allen and Tudor Humphries

KING*f*ISHER

Are you a bee?

Perhaps you are a honeybee?
If so, your mother is a queen.
She looks like this and she
lays eggs.

Your life began inside one of her eggs.

When you hatch, you are not a pretty sight.

You are a grub.

You are in a small room with six walls. It's called a cell.

Your older sisters bring food.
Eat it and grow.

Grow until you fill your cell.

One of your older sisters puts
a wax ceiling on your cell.

In your closed cell you change
a lot more.

When you are ready, chew a hole
in the ceiling and climb out.

NOW you look like a bee.

You have a hairy body, with stripes,
six legs and four wings.
You have two feelers on your head.
You have a sting.

You are not alone. You have
a few hundred brothers and
thousands of sisters.

You live in a nest built by your older sisters.

Your nest might be in a hollow tree.

It might hang down from
a tree branch.

Most likely it will
be inside a hive.

Your brothers
are drones.
They don't do much.

You and your sisters
are workers.
You do everything.

You clean the nest,
feed the grubs, look after
the queen and build new cells.

You fan the nest
with your wings to
cool it in summer.

You guard the nest to keep
out strange bees.

Busy, busy, busy.

Leave the nest and
fetch food from flowers.

How will you know
where to look?

Your sisters will
make up a dance to tell you.

Watch the dance carefully.
  Don't worry, you'll understand it –

              you're a **bee.**

There is sweet liquid in flowers. It's called nectar and it's hidden deep inside. This is not a problem. You have a long tongue, you can reach it.

Also, you have a special stomach to carry it in. You'll get pollen-dust all over you. Scrape it off with your front legs and put it in the pollen-baskets on your back legs.

When you get home,
your sisters will help
you put the nectar and
the pollen into store-cells.
Mix some of the nectar
with pollen to make
bee-bread.

Leave the rest of the
nectar to turn into honey.

Bee-bread is good to eat.
So is honey.

If you find a new patch
of flowers, be sure to tell
your sisters.

How?
Dance of course!

More eggs hatch.
More grubs turn into bees.
Soon there isn't enough room.
What will happen next?

Your mother,
the old queen, leaves.

She takes you and a lot
of your sisters with her.

Deep in the nest a royal grub is hatching. She is in a different kind of cell and she is fed on rich food called royal jelly. When she becomes a bee, she is a young queen.

She flies away and mates with drones from another nest so that she can lay eggs. When she flies home again, she is the new queen.

Fly with your sisters - follow
the old queen.

Keep together - you are part of a swarm.
When the queen stops,
swarm around her.

Now you must build a new
nest – but where?

Maybe the queen will send
scout-bees to find a good place.

Or maybe a beekeeper will find you and take you all to an empty hive.

Why is the beekeeper dressed like this?

In case you get flustered and try to sting.

However,

if your mother looks
a bit like this   or this

or this

you are not a bee.

You are...

25

...a human child.

You haven't got a hairy body
with stripes on it.

You haven't got a long tongue.

You haven't got a sting.

Also, it is very unlikely that you have hundreds of brothers and thousands of sisters.

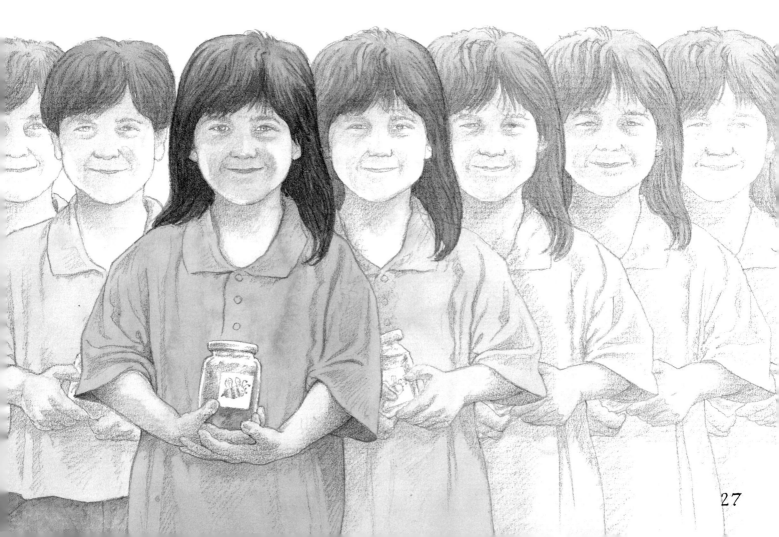

Never mind, you can do a great
many things a bee can't do.

You can still eat bread and honey,
but you'll never have to fetch
your food from flowers.

Best of all,
you don't have
to be busy, busy,
busy all day long.

Did You Know...

...bees are happy to live in a hive because the beekeeper has already built part of the nest for them. If bees live in a hollow tree, they have to build the whole nest themselves.

...a worker bee can sting only once, then it dies, but a queen bee can sting many times.

...bees carry pollen on their furry bodies from flower to flower. The pollen from one flower rubs off onto others to make seeds that will grow into new plants.

...the average worker bee makes one-and-a-half teaspoonfuls of honey in her lifetime.